More Animal Tales and Legends

A Dolch Classic Basic Reading Book

by Edward W. Dolch and Marguerite P. Dolch

illustrated by Kersti Frigell

The Basic Reading Books

The Basic Reading Books are fun reading books that fill the need for easy-to-read stories for the primary grades. The interest appeal of these folktales and legends will encourage independent reading at the early reading levels.

The stories focus on the 95 Common Nouns and the Dolch 220 Basic Sight Vocabulary. Beyond these simple lists, the books use about two or three new words per page.

This series was prepared under the direction and supervision of Edward W. Dolch, Ph.D.

This revision was prepared under the direction and supervision of Eleanor Dolch LaRoy and the Dolch Family Trust.

SRA/McGraw-Hill

A Division of The **McGraw·Hill** Companies

Original version copyright © 1958 by Edward W. Dolch.
Copyright © 1999 by SRA/McGraw-Hill. All rights reserved.
Except as permitted under the United States Copyright Act, no part of this publication may be reproduced or distributed in any form or by any means, or stored in a database or retrieval system without prior written permission from the publisher.

Printed in the United States of America.

Send all inquiries to:
SRA/McGraw-Hill
250 Old Wilson Bridge Road, Suite 310
Worthington, OH 43085

ISBN 0-02-830813-1

2 3 4 5 6 7 8 9 0 QST 04 03 02 01 00 99

Table of Contents

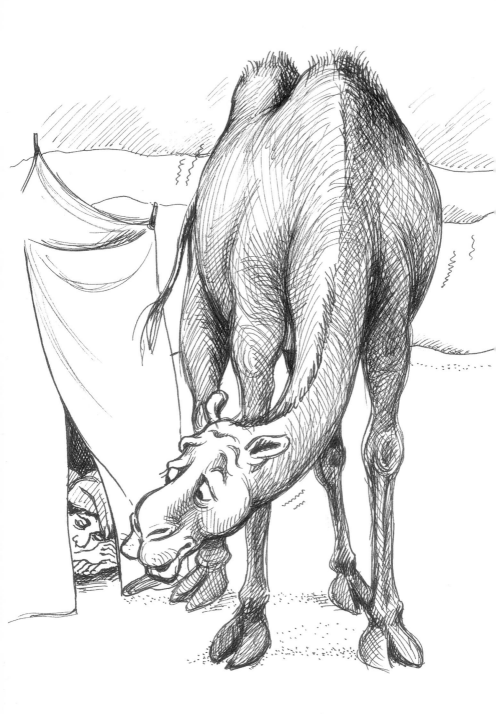

The Camel and the Tent

There is an old saying in the Middle East, "Never let a camel get his head into your tent."

In the Middle East it is very hot in the day time and very cold at night. And in the Middle East you must sometimes ride upon a camel.

Then when the sun goes down, you would put up a tent to sleep in.

One night a man was sleeping inside his tent. His camel was on the outside. And the camel got cold.

"My Kind Master," said the camel, "all day I have carried you on my back. I am very tired, but I cannot go to sleep."

The man sat up and said, "I thought that I heard my camel talking to me."

"Kind Master, it is I, your camel, who is talking to you. I am outside your tent and the night is very cold."

"And what do you want?" asked the man.

"Kind Master," said the camel, "let me put my head inside your tent. Then I can go to sleep."

"You are a good camel," said the man. "Put your head inside my tent, and we will both go to sleep."

And so the camel put his head inside the tent. And the man went to sleep again.

Pretty soon the camel said, "Kind Master, I cannot go to sleep. My legs are very cold. If I could only put my front legs inside your tent, I could go to sleep."

The man was very sleepy and he said, "Yes, yes, put your front legs inside the tent, and let us both go to sleep."

And so the camel put his front legs inside the tent. And the man went to sleep again.

Before long, the camel said, "Kind Master, I cannot go to sleep. My head and my front legs are warm. But my back and my back legs are cold, and I cannot go to sleep. Please, Kind Master, may I put them inside your tent?"

The man was very sleepy and he said, "Yes, yes, put them in and let us both go to sleep." Now it was just a little tent. The camel's head and his front legs were inside the tent. He put his back and his back legs inside the tent.

The camel said to himself, "Both of us can never sleep in this tent." He pushed and he pushed and he pushed the man right out of the tent into the cold night. Then the camel went to sleep in the man's tent.

And that is why they say in the Middle East, "Never let a camel get his head into your tent."

The Ape and the Firefly

The ape is the very biggest of the monkeys. He is very big, and the firefly is very little.

One night an ape was looking at the fireflies flying about. They were lighting their little lights and then putting them out, and then lighting them again and then putting them out.

The fireflies looked very pretty. The apes thought he would have some fun with them. So he said to the biggest firefly, "Mr. Firefly, I would like you to tell me why you always carry a light."

"I show my light so that the mosquitoes will not hurt me," said the firefly.

"Ho, ho, ho," laughed the ape. "You are afraid of the mosquitoes."

"I am not afraid of the mosquitoes," said the firefly. "I show my light because I do not want the mosquitoes to hurt me."

"You are a coward," said the ape. "I think you are afraid of the mosquitoes."

"I am not a coward," said the firefly.

The ape laughed at the firefly. Then he said to the other apes that the firefly was a coward because he was afraid of the mosquitoes.

"I will show you that I am not a coward," said the firefly. "Will you fight with me tomorrow night?"

The big ape laughed. And all the other apes laughed. It was very funny that a firefly wanted to fight an ape.

"You had better bring all the other fireflies to help you," said the ape. "And I will bring some other apes to help me, Mr. Firefly."

All the apes laughed and laughed. It was very funny that it would take many big apes to fight a little thing like a firefly.

"Bring as many apes with you as you want," said the firefly. "Tomorrow night I will show you that I am no coward."

The next night ten big apes came. Each ape had a big stick.

"Do you want to fight," asked the big ape.

"Yes," said the firefly. "I do. And I shall show you that I am not a coward."

"Where are the other fireflies that are going to help you?" asked the big ape.

"The other fireflies are watching from the trees," said the firefly. "They do not have to help me fight you apes."

The firefly sat on the big ape's nose. The next ape tried to hit the firefly with his stick, but the firefly jumped and the stick came down on the big ape's nose. The ape cried out because his nose hurt very much. He ran away into the woods.

Then the firefly showed his light again. He sat down on another ape's nose. Another ape tried to hit the firefly with his stick. But the firefly jumped, and the stick came down on the ape's nose. That ape ran away into the woods.

And so it went. The firefly showed his light and sat on an ape's nose. Another ape tried to hit the firefly, but the firefly jumped and the stick came down on the ape's nose. In no time at all, all the apes were running into the woods, crying because their noses were hurting very, very much.

Then all the fireflies came out of the trees and showed their lights. They laughed and laughed at the apes.

The fireflies called after the apes, "Never again say that a firefly is a coward."

Now when night comes and the fireflies show their lights, the apes run away into the woods. No ape wants a firefly to sit on his nose.

The Four Friends

Once upon a time a crow and a rat and a turtle were very good friends. The crow lived in a tree. The rat lived in the woods in a hole. But the turtle liked the water, and so he lived in a pond in the woods.

The crow and the rat and the turtle saw a goat running in the woods. The goat was running very fast.

"Some hunter is trying to get the goat," said the crow. "Friend Turtle, go down into the water of the pond. Friend Rat, go down into your hole. And I will fly up into the tree. The hunter will not get us."

The goat went to the pond. She looked all around. Then she took a big drink of the cold water.

The turtle put his head out of the
pond and said, "Friend Goat, why were
you running so fast?"

"The hunter wanted to get me," said the goat, "but I ran fast and got away."

The crow came down from his tree, and the rat came out of his hole.

"Friend Goat," said the crow, "why don't you live in the woods with us? We will be your friends."

"Yes," said the rat, "you would like to live in the woods."

"Yes," said the turtle, "we can all live together in the woods."

"I would like to live in the woods," said the goat. "Then we could all look out for that hunter."

And so the four friends lived in the woods together.

One day when the rat and the crow went to the pond in the woods, the turtle said, "Where is Friend Goat today? Do you think that the hunter could have found our friend Goat?"

"I will fly up into the tree and look all around," said the crow.

The crow flew up to the top of a big tree and looked all around. And then the crow flew down to the pond and said, "I saw our friend Goat, and she is in a net that the hunter put in the grass."

"We must go to her right away," said the rat. "We must get her out of that net before the hunter comes back and kills our friend Goat."

"Friend Rat, I will take you to where Friend Goat is in the net," said the crow. And the crow took hold of the rat's tail and flew with him to where the goat was in the net.

The rat cut the net with his teeth, and soon the goat was out of the net.

"Oh, thank you my good friends," said the goat. "And now we must run away very fast before the hunter comes."

But just then they saw the turtle in the grass.

"Friend Turtle, why did you come?" said the goat. "If the hunter comes now, you cannot run very fast on your little legs."

And then the hunter came to see whether the goat was in his net.

The goat ran away very fast. And the crow flew up in a tree. The rat found a hole and ran into it. But the turtle could not get away.

"Now how did that goat get out of my net," said the hunter to himself. And he looked all around. Then he saw the turtle in the grass.

"A turtle is better than nothing," said the hunter, and he put the turtle in a bag and started back to his house.

The crow flew down from the tree. The rat came out of the hole. And the goat ran back.

"What are we to do," said the rat.

"The hunter is going to eat our friend turtle," said the crow.

"I will run before the hunter," said the goat. "Then he will put down his bag and run after me."

And that is just what the goat did. When the hunter saw the goat, he put down his bag and ran after the goat. The goat ran as fast as she could. And the hunter ran and ran and tried to get the goat.

The rat ran to the bag and cut a hole in it. The turtle got out of the bag. He went back to the pond in the woods as fast as he could go. The rat ran back to his hole in the ground. And the crow flew up to his nest in the tree.

The goat ran so fast that the hunter could not get him. Pretty soon the hunter went back to where he had put down his bag on the grass. He found a hole in the bag, and he found that the turtle was not in the bag.

"This is a sad day for me," said the hunter to himself. "I had a goat in my net and it got away. I had a turtle in my bag and it got away. And now I will have nothing to eat but bread."

And so the hunter went back to his house.

The four friends went to the pond in the woods and talked together.

And the four friends said, "As long as we shall live, we shall help one another." And the crow and the rat and the turtle and the goat lived in the woods a long, long time.

The Big Moose

Once upon a time, a moose went to
the river to drink. He was a big, big
moose. The big moose began to drink
and drink. The water in the river began
to go down.

There was a beaver who had his house in the river. When the water in the river began to go down, the beaver was afraid. He was afraid that there would be no water around his house.

The beaver ran into the woods. He saw a rabbit.

"Oh, Mr. Rabbit," cried the beaver, "come and help me. Make the big moose go away. He is drinking all the water in the river. There will be no water around my house."

The rabbit was afraid of the big, big moose. He looked this way and he looked that way. Then the rabbit said to the beaver, "Mr. Beaver, I would help you if I could, but I must be going."

The rabbit ran off into the woods as fast as he could go.

Pretty soon the beaver saw a bear.

"Oh, Mr. Bear," cried the beaver. "Come and help me. Make the big moose go away. He is drinking all the water in the river. There will be no water around my house."

The bear was afraid of the big moose. He looked very sleepy, and he said to the beaver, "Mr. Beaver, I would help you if I could, but I am just going to sleep."

Pretty soon the beaver saw a fox. "Oh, Mrs. Fox," cried the beaver. "Make the big moose go away. He is drinking all the water in the river. There will be no water around my house."

The fox was afraid of the big Moose. She looked this way, and she looked that way. Then the fox said to the beaver, "Mr. Beaver, I would help you if I could, but I have much work to do. I have no time to go to the river."

The fox ran off into the woods.

The beaver could not get anyone to help him. So he went back to the river.

All this time the big moose had been drinking the water out of the river. The water in the river was going down and down and down.

The fish in the river were afraid. They were afraid that there would be no water in the river for them to swim in.

One of the little fish saw a little fly.

"Little fly, little fly," said the fish. "Come and help us. Come and help us. Make the big moose go away from the river. Make the big moose go away."

"I will try. I will try," said the little fly. "I am not afraid of the big moose. I will make him go away from the river."

The little fly flew up to the big moose. He bit the big moose on the leg.

"Go away. Go away," cried the big moose. "Do not bite me. Do not bite me."

The little fly flew up on the back of the big moose. He bit the big moose here. He bit the big moose there. The big moose turned this way. The big moose turned that way.

"Go away. Go away," cried the big moose. "Do not bite me. Do not bite me."

But the big moose could not get the little fly to go away.

The little fly flew to the nose of the big moose. He bit the big moose here. He bit the big moose there. The big moose turned this way. The big moose turned that way, but he could not get the little fly to go away.

The big moose ran away into the woods.

"Thank you, little fly," said the fish. "You made the big moose go away."

"Thank you, little fly," said the beaver. "You were the only one that would help us. You made the big moose go away."

And the little fly said, "Who is afraid of a big, big moose?"

The Hungry Wolf

There was once a very hungry wolf. One day he went off to see whether he could find something to eat.

The first animal that he saw was a goat. The wolf went up to the goat and said, "Mr. Goat, I am going to eat you because I am a hungry wolf."

"What a funny-looking wolf you are," said the goat. "I say that you are nothing but a big dog."

"No, no," said the wolf, "I am not a dog. I am a hungry wolf."

"If you are a hungry wolf," said the goat, "I will run down the hill and jump into your mouth."

"All right," said the wolf, and he opened his mouth.

The goat ran down the hill, and he
hit that wolf hard. The wolf went over
and over right down the hill. Then the
goat ran away.

The wolf got up and his head hurt
very much.

"What a fool I was to open my
mouth like that," said the wolf to
himself. "I never heard of a goat jumping
into anyone's mouth."

The wolf got up and went on his way, but he was very hungry. Then the wolf saw a horse.

"Mr. Horse," said the wolf, "I am going to eat you because I am a hungry wolf."

"What a funny-looking wolf you are," said the Horse. "I do not think that you are a wolf at all. I say that you are nothing but a big dog."

"No, no," said the wolf, "I am going to eat you."

"Well, if you are going to eat me," said the horse, "let me eat the green grass as long as I can for the grass makes me grow."

"All right," said the wolf, "eat as much grass as you like."

"Thank you," said the horse. "And now if you are going to eat me, you had better start eating my tail first."

So the wolf went around to the back of the horse. He was just going to start to eat the horse's tail when up went the horse's two back feet. And the wolf went over and over on his head.

The horse laughed and ran away as fast as he could.

The wolf got up. His head hurt him very much.

"What a fool I was," said the wolf to himself. "I never heard of anyone starting to eat a horse by the tail. I should have known that the horse would kick me with his two back feet."

The wolf went on his way, but he was very, very hungry. Then the wolf saw a pig.

"Mr. Pig," said the wolf, "I am going to eat you because I am a hungry wolf."

"What a funny-looking wolf you are," said the pig. "I do not think that you are a wolf at all. I say that you are nothing but a big dog."

"No, no," said the wolf, "I am not a dog. I am a hungry wolf."

"Well, if you are a wolf, that is all right with me," said the pig. "Jump on my back and I will give you a ride, and then you can eat me."

And so the wolf jumped on the pig's back. Off ran the pig as fast as he could go. The pig ran down the road and ran right to the farmer's house.

All the dogs on the farm came running to see the old wolf riding on the pig's back. The wolf jumped off the pig's back and ran away to the woods as fast as he could.

"I think I will eat bread," said the wolf, "or I will get nothing to eat today."

The Rabbit and the Monkey

Once upon a time a rabbit and a monkey were sitting by the road. A man came down the road carrying a basket of bananas.

Now the monkey liked to eat bananas, so he said to the rabbit, "Friend Rabbit, if you will sit in the road, the man will put down his basket of bananas and run after you. Then I will get the basket of bananas and take it up into a tree."

The rabbit sat in the road. The man put down his basket of bananas and ran after him. But the rabbit ran away so fast that the man did not get him.

The monkey got the basket of bananas and went up into a tree. He sat up in the tree and one by one, he ate all of the bananas in the basket.

When the man came back, he looked all around but he could not find his basket of bananas. So he went home with no bananas for his children.

Soon the rabbit came and called to the monkey, "Come down from the tree, Friend Monkey, and we will eat the bananas."

But the monkey would not come down from the tree.

"Give me some of the bananas," said the rabbit.

"There are no bananas," said the monkey.

"You have the bananas in the basket," said the rabbit, "and I want you to give some of them to me."

The monkey only laughed. He went down, and he took hold of the rabbit's long ears. He pulled him up into the tree. Then he said, "Friend Rabbit, look into the basket if you want to. You will find no bananas there." And then the monkey laughed and ran away.

The rabbit did not know what to do. He would get hurt if he tried to jump down from the tree.

A cow came by and the rabbit called, "Friend Cow, will you please help me get down from the tree?" But the cow went on down the road.

A horse came by and the rabbit called, "Friend Horse, will you please help me get down from this tree?" But the horse went on down the road.

The rabbit sat up in the tree a long, long time. And then a big elephant came down the road.

"Friend Elephant," called the rabbit, "Will you please help me get down from the tree?"

The big elephant stopped.

"Come under the tree," said the rabbit, "and then I can jump down onto your back."

"Yes," said the big elephant. "I will help you because you are little and I am big. I like to help because I am the elephant that helps the king."

And so the elephant went up to the tree, and the rabbit jumped down on the elephant's back.

"I have always wanted to see the palace of the king," said the rabbit.

"Ride on my back," said the big elephant, "and I will take you to the palace of the king."

And the elephant went on down the road with the rabbit on his back. Pretty soon, they got to the palace of the king.

"Go right in," said the big elephant. "But do not let the men at the door see you."

And so the rabbit went into the palace of the king. He went and sat under the king's chair.

Pretty soon the king and all his men came in. The king sat down in his chair.

And then the rabbit under the king's chair sneezed a big sneeze.

The king called, "Who sneezes before the king?"

But no one knew who had sneezed.

Then the rabbit under the king's chair sneezed a big sneeze again.

This time the men knew that the sneeze came from under the king's chair. They pulled the rabbit out.

The king said, "Did you sneeze before the king?"

And the rabbit said, "I could not help it."

And the men cried, "Off with his head."

"Please. Oh, my king, do not cut off my head," cried the rabbit. "I will take you to see a big elephant."

"What," cried the king. "You know where my big elephant can be found? My men have looked for him all day and have not found him."

"Yes," said the rabbit. "I will take you to your big elephant."

And so the king and the rabbit went out of the palace. And there was the big elephant by the door. The king was so pleased to have his elephant back that he gave the rabbit a red coat and a big horse to ride.

The rabbit put on the red coat. He got up on the big horse and he went riding down the road.

And there on the road he saw the monkey.

"Friend Rabbit," called the monkey, "where did you get that red coat and that big horse?"

"The king gave them to me," said the rabbit, "because I sneezed under his chair." And the rabbit went down the road on his big horse.

"I would like to have a red coat and a big horse like the rabbit has," said the monkey to himself. "I will go and sneeze under the king's chair."

The monkey ran to the palace. He went into the palace and got under the chair of the king.

Pretty soon the king and all his men came in. The king sat down in his chair.

And then the monkey under the chair sneezed a big sneeze.

The king cried, "Who sneezed before the king?

Then one of the king's men pulled the monkey out from under the chair.

The king said, "Did you sneeze before the king?"

"Yes," said the monkey. "And I would like a red coat and a big horse."

"Off with his head," cried the king's men.

"No," said the king. "It is only a monkey. Just put him into the river."

The king's men threw the monkey into the river.

As the monkey was coming out of the river, the rabbit came down the road in his red coat and on his big horse.

"Now how are you today, Friend Monkey?" asked the rabbit. "And how did you get into the river?"

"I went into the palace," said the monkey. "I sneezed under the chair of the king. But the king did not give me a red coat and a big horse. His men threw me into the river."

The rabbit laughed and laughed.

"You did not sneeze the right way, Friend Monkey," said the rabbit, "because you were too full of bananas."

And the rabbit in his red coat went down the road on his big horse.

The Bell of Atri

In a town called Atri, there lived a good king. He was kind to his people. He wanted all of his people to do what was right.

One day the king had his men put up a big bell in the town of Atri. They tied a long rope onto the bell, and all the people came to see the big bell.

"What is the king going to do with the big bell," the people asked. But the king's people did not know.

Pretty soon the king came riding up on his white horse.

The people all said, "Now the king will ring the big bell." But the king did not ring the bell.

The king sat on his white horse and he talked to the people.

"My people," said the king, "I want only the good and the right things for all of you. If you think that you have been wronged, come and ring this big bell. Then I, the king, will come, and try to right the wrong."

For a long, long time no one in the town of Atri made the big bell ring. The rope on the bell was so old that some of it had fallen away.

One day one of the king's people saw that no one could ring the big bell of Atri because they could not get hold of the old rope. So the man tied a long vine onto the rope, and he went away to get a long, new rope to put on the bell.

Outside the town of Atri, there lived a man on a farm. He had much money, and he had many horses and cows and sheep. But he was not a kind man, and he had a very old horse who was too old to work any more.

One day this man said to himself, "That old horse cannot work for me now. I will not give him anything more to eat. Let him eat the grass that grows by the road."

So the old man took a big stick and made the old horse go away from the farm where he had worked so long.

The old horse walked down the road, but he did not find much grass to eat. At last the old horse walked into the town of Atri.

The old horse walked up to the bell that the king had put up, and there the horse saw the vine tied to the rope of the bell. There were green leaves on the vine and the old horse began to eat them. He pulled and he pulled at the green leaves.

As the old horse pulled at the leaves, he pulled the rope that was on the bell.

The big bell of Atri started to ring and ring.

The people came running. They had not heard the big bell of Atri ring for a long, long time. The people laughed and laughed when they saw the old horse ring the bell.

The king came riding up on his white horse, but the king did not laugh.

"Someone has made this old horse go away from his home because he is too old to work," said the king. "Go and bring the man who owns this horse to me. This horse has made the bell of Atri ring so that I, the king, may right a wrong."

The king's men went and got the old man. And the king said to him, "Is this your horse?"

And the old man said, "Yes."

"Has this horse worked hard for you?" asked the king.

And the old man said, "Yes."

"You did wrong to make this old horse go away from your farm," said the king. "He has worked hard for you. You are to give this horse something to eat every day as long as he lives."

And so the man took the old horse back to the farm.

And the king said to his people, "I will always try to right a wrong for the one who rings the bell of Atri, even if it is a horse."

Monkey and the Leopard

Wise old Monkey sat up in a tree. He looked down and saw Leopard sleeping in the grass.

"Leopard would like to eat me," thought Monkey.

Just then Leopard opened his eyes. He thought to himself, "I am so hungry. If a monkey came by, I would eat him."

Someone began to laugh.

"Come and let me see who is laughing," said Leopard.

Wise old Monkey in the tree laughed again. "Foolish Leopard," he said, "do you think that I would go near you?"

Leopard thought and then he said, "Monkey, would you please help me?

I have a thorn in my foot. With this thorn in my foot, I can get nothing to eat. You are wise. You can pull the thorn out of my foot. Please come down and help me."

"I wish I could help you," said Monkey, but he knew that Leopard was playing a trick.

"Please help me," said Leopard. "If you will help me, I will tell all the leopards to be friends with the monkeys."

"I would like to come down," said Monkey. "But I cannot move. My tail is caught in the tree."

As soon as Monkey said this, Leopard jumped up.

"Now I will eat you, you foolish Monkey. I did not know that your tail was caught."

Leopard climbed up the tree to get Monkey. But Monkey just climbed higher and higher up into the tree.

Monkey called back to Leopard, "I am not a foolish monkey. My tail was not caught at all. And you did not have a thorn in your foot. When you try to trick others, you can be tricked yourself."

a
about
afraid
after
again
all
always
am
an
and
animal
another
any
anyone
anyone's
anything
ape
apes
ape's
are
around
as
asked
at
ate
Atri
away
back
bag
bananas
basket
be
bear
beaver
because
been
before

began
bell
better
big
biggest
bit
bite
both
bread
bring
but
by
called
came
camel
camel's
can
cannot
carried
carry
carrying
caught
chair
children
climbed
coat
cold
come
comes
coming
could
cow
coward
cows
cried
crow
crying

cut
day
did
do
dog
dogs
don't
door
down
drink
drinking
each
ears
east
eat
eating
elephant
elephant's
even
every
eyes
fallen
farm
farmer's
fast
feet
fight
find
fireflies
firefly
first
fish
flew
fly
flying
fool
foolish

foot
for
found
four
fox
friend
friends
from
front
full
fun
funny
gave
get
give
go
goat
goes
going
good
got
grass
green
ground
grow
grows
had
hard
has
have
he
head
heard
help
helps
her
here

higher
hill
him
himself
his
hit
ho
hold
hole
home
horse
horses
horse's
hot
house
how
hungry
hunter
hurt
hurting
I
if
in
inside
into
is
it
jump
jumped
jumping
just
kick
kills
kind
king
king's
knew

know
known
last
laugh
laughed
laughing
leaves
leg
legs
leopard
leopards
let
light
lighting
lights
like
liked
little
live
lived
lives
long
look
looked
looking
made
make
makes
man
man's
many
master
may
me
men
middle
money

monkey
monkeys
moose
more
mosquitoes
mouth
move
Mr.
Mrs.
much
must
my
near
nest
net
never
new
next
night
no
noose
nose
noses
not
nothing
now
of
off
oh
old
on
once
one
only
onto
open
opened

or
other
others
our
out
outside
over
owns
palace
people
pig
pig's
playing
please
pleased
pond
pretty
pull
pulled
pushed
put
putting
rabbit
rabbit's
ran
rat
rat's
red
ride
riding
right
ring
ringing
rings
river
road
rope

run
running
sad
said
sat
saw
say
saying
see
shall
she
sheep
should
show
showed
sit
sitting
sleep
sleeping
sleepy
sneeze
sneezed
sneezes
so
some
someone
something
sometimes
soon
start
started
starting
stick
stopped
sun
swim
tail

take
talked
talking
teeth
tell
ten
tent
than
thank
that
the
their
them
then
there
they
thing
things
think
this
thorn
thought
threw
throw
tied
time
tired
to
today
together
tomorrow
too
took
top
town
tree
trees

trick
tricked
tried
try
trying
turn
turned
turtle
two
under
up
upon
us
very
vine
walked
want
wanted
wants
warm
was
watching
water
way
we
well

went
were
what
when
where
whether
white
who
why
will
wise
wish
with
wolf
woods
work
worked
would
wrong
wronged
yes
you
your
yourself